SHED MEN

GARETH JONES

SHED MEN

CONTENTS

THE ORIGINS OF THE SHED

It begins in boyhood and the bedroom. Think Steptoe's yard meets crime scene and you're close to describing the territory – ridges of dirty clothes, scree-slopes of magazines and CDs, crop-circles of plates and mugs. There is only a door standing between this scene of utter madness and the outside world, between Mum and Dad's guests and the complex odour of fermenting socks and half-eaten ham sandwiches.

Mum doesn't understand why he chooses to live this way. Sometimes she gets a bit emotional about it. She racks her brains for reasons, and blames herself. Was it something to do with that time when she lost him in ASDA when he was three? Meanwhile, he positively revels in the mess. It is a statement of his non-conformity, identity, ownership. The room is his to do with as he wishes, the door is his to close, his to slam.

The years pass. The mess remains, though the composition changes, reflecting each new hobby or interest. Boy becomes man, meets girl, settles down. Threatened with the removal of certain privileges, he mends his ways and grudgingly boxes up his collection of matchbox labels, his copies of *Razzle*, and the bleached dog skull he sneaked back from holiday when he was twelve.

6

Suddenly he is a refugee, his emotional clutter homeless, his personal space compromised. The next, most natural home for this "space" is the bottom of the garden – that shady place where he used to grub for worms or deeper, more mysterious objects.

SHEDS AND SHEDDISM

A shed in its most typical form is a simple, outdoor structure comprising roof, walls and an entrance of some sort – a definition covering everything from a humble outdoor privy to a farmer's barn. "Sheddism" is a movement which has adopted the shed as a construct or metaphor for the personal, creative space it contains – that is, everything from a scientist's robot to a bloke's model railway.

Some men even adopt an alternative territory, but refer to it as their "shed", be it a study, box room, attic, basement or garage. The majority of these "sheds" are located on the edge of the domestic sphere, indicating a straining towards the outside, and all usually have a door of some sort, to protect the occupant from the outside world, and vice versa. The shed phenomenon has even gone 21st century, with a wealth of virtual sheds on the internet, or websites such as www.readersheds.com where you are invited to "share your shed".

But perhaps the most necessary definition is this: a shed is like televised test-match cricket. Both provide a watertight excuse for a man to sit around all weekend, daydreaming and drinking beer, rather than sanding the sharp edges off the baby's cot or replacing the broken smoke alarm.

SHEDDISM VS FEMINISM

One school of shedological thought views a bloke's shed simply as a means of hiding away from the world and the other half.

There are other advantages though. The time he spends in a shed offers the illusion of industriousness, whether he really is building that coffee table or simply daydreaming and drinking beer. Then there is the simple pleasure of making and fixing. The process often becomes more rewarding than the finished object itself, and so the shed dweller adds components here and modifications there – all of which, he will insist, are crucial, regardless of whether or not the original coffee table design included a series of ornate gargoyle carvings.

In fact, the pleasures of sheds are such that a growing number of ladies are experiencing "shed envy" and getting in on the shed action themselves.

THE FUTURE FOR THE SHED

Like poetry, bingo and gardening before it, sheddism is the new rock 'n' roll. It's on the TV, in the weekend papers, there are even books on it. People are talking about it on the bus, down the pub, at the opera, in the waiting rooms of maternity wards. A group of people even put their religion down on the last UK census as "Shedi", and when you think about it, it all makes sense. What is a church, mosque, temple or other place of worship apart from a very big shed where a lot of people come to pay their homage?

The shed was selected as a Millennium icon, has had a recent "Shed Summit" devoted to it, and apparently an average of one shed is purchased every ten minutes – that's almost as frequent as a performance of *Hamlet* somewhere in the world. So what does the future hold for sheds and sheddism? Well, sheddists tell me that, amongst other things, we will all live in sheds, degrees in shedology will be offered by universities across the land, and there will be Government-funded research on the subject. Shedman will embrace shedman and the world will be happy, the world will be sheddy.

Gareth Jones

A PLACE TO DREAM A BIT

Derek's shed was originally used to keep chickens and goats. Now it's home to a number of his projects – the fruits of a wonderful imagination and a long career as a mechanical design engineer. The fin-shaped device is his safe alternative to a conventional propeller: it works in an up-and-down motion, like a fish's tail.

His affinity with sheds goes back some way. During the '70s, he was part of a team that developed a pedal-powered aeroplane. It could be dismantled to fit through a standard 30-inch-wide door, but it had a 136 foot wingspan, and they had nowhere to keep it, until some bright spark hit on the idea of erecting two pre-fabs end-to-end and knocking through.

Derek's latest set-up is a bit more permanent, though his design work has had to take second place to maintenance. "I spent most of last winter positioning buckets to catch the drips through the roof. It's still coming into the house, but I think I've got the shed sorted."

10

"Most of the firms I worked for went bust."

THE SECRET OF A SUCCESSFUL MARRIAGE

For Bryan, a shared interest is the key. "If your wife disagrees with the thing you like most, it wouldn't work. You've got to do it together…" As Bryan's model railway takes up the whole garden, it's good that his wife Sandra is happy for him to maintain the tracks and rolling stock while she looks after the flowers, which tower like triffids over the passengers on the platforms. "You do have your ups and downs… Like when a train hits one of her plants and runs off the tracks." Come rain or shine they're out there, even during the winter months. And there's no such thing as the wrong kind of snow – Bryan has a concrete-laden plough to clear the rails.

His shed's the hub of the operation. It's the control room and contains all the tools he needs for repairs, plus a regiment of old Brylcreem pots, which contain "proper" sheddy stuff like nails and screws. "What I really could've done with is a bigger shed – a two-tier job with the track running around the bottom and the operating side in the top half… I don't think I could have got planning permission – it'd be 20 foot high."

"You get married to your shed as well."

AN EVENING AT GUZZLE-DOWN LODGE

In its previous incarnation, Guzzle-Down Lodge was a summerhouse – one half functioning as a kid's playhouse, the other side as an aviary. It wasn't getting used a great deal, apart from Ken (with mic) and others – like brother Lol, Doug and Colin – sitting around the table. Ken would find himself traipsing back to the house for fresh supplies every few minutes; a "little brainwave" led him to install a bar in the corner.

"It sort of went from one extreme to the other," he says, sheepishly. The hostelry now boasts lasers, smoke machine, disco lights, two-screen karaoke machine... oh, and beer on tap. Car-boot purchases and gifts from the regulars have provided visual interest: a plaque his wife bought him even inspired the name.

Aside from special occasions, such as the annual New Year's Eve bash and the family lunch on Christmas Day, Ken now plays host and MC roughly once a month. "We have music till about 11 o'clock and then everyone starts screaming for karaoke... That normally finishes about 4 o'clock in the morning."

"It's got everything that a nightclub's got, really."

THE BEST CURRACH HOUSE IN TOWN

Holger was involved in collaborative research between the Eden project and Falmouth College of Art, examining traditional crafts and sustainable plant materials, and bringing those elements into architecture. He found inspiration in the Irish currach – a mode of water transport similar to the coracle. "The boat is like a container when you're on the water. But on land you'd turn it around and then it's like a shelter."

Taking this traditional craft, he added a pinch of modern architecture, incorporating a row of windows beneath the roof, and elements that open up to let the light in and compensate for the dark materials the shed is made from. "The roof is made from woven hazel rods, like a Boyne river currach. The rest of the shed is made of willow rods, changing the design a little bit."

Holger gave it to Katie and Sara, a ceramic designer and a photographer. The pair have given it a particularly fitting home – an allotment close to the sea. "It looks great. Sitting on the hill, it really sticks out."

"All the other sheds are ordinary, little, rough-looking thingies."

TONY'S TIGER SHED

Tony's garden shed is a museum dedicated to tiger artefacts amassed from countries across the world. Everyone he knows is on the look-out for tigers wherever they go. His daughter is particularly good at tracking them down. "She travels a lot and always has her eye open."

Sitting whisker by jowl alongside Guatemalan figurines, Mexican masks and Japanese clockwork models are a number of pieces Tony has commissioned from local artists. He even has a 9-foot long fibreglass tiger from the Bridgwater Festival. "We stuck it in the car and I had to lie horizontal with the tiger in the front seat as we drove along the motorway... It caused quite a few raised eyebrows."

Tony's wife is involved with local education and they have parties of school children round to visit. A trail of tiger footprints leads them from the road over walls and dustbins to the shed. "The teacher then sits on the tiger chair and reads the children a story while they wear the little tiger tails my wife makes for them."

"I don't collect cuddly toys."

AS TIME WHIPS BY

James discovered the joy of metal at the tender age of 14. On his first day as an engineer he was put to work on a lathe and the rest just followed. "I've enjoyed my life as an engineer. I look back and I've been paid for a pleasure."

James enjoyed it so much, in fact, that he'd soon built himself a shed and kitted it out with all the tools an engineer could need, making as much of the machinery as he could with a blend of scrap metal and love. Word soon got around and he became the street's knife sharpener and car mechanic. "I found if you did something for free you were always passed on to someone else."

He made toys for the children – jigsaws, dolls' houses, even a go-kart modelled on a Rolls Royce. Recent projects include a tune-playing scale-model barrel organ and a fully working mini spinning wheel, as well as paintings and poems. "As I'm working my mind sort of wanders... The only thing is that time just whips by."

"I've tried to spin on it but it's too small."

SHED DELAYS MILLION-METRE-CLUB MEMBERSHIP

The old shed collapsed. Gordon's wife needed "somewhere to put the mower where it won't get wet." Soon afterwards, on a trip to review and photograph a jazz festival in the States, he came across what's known over there as a "backyard barn". Inspired, he tracked down plans on the internet, only to discover that across the pond they still use imperial measurements and have their own terminology for things like nails.

But, determined as he was, he put all his energies into it for six weeks, even putting off his goal of reaching a million metres on his indoor rower. "If you reach a million, they send you a free T-shirt." He even adapted the plans to incorporate a secret entrance at the back for his granddaughters, India and Mali. "It's 3 foot high and opens up on to the trees at the back of our garden."

So everyone was happy? "My wife's comment at the end of it all was, 'It's too good. I'm not sure I can put a mower in there.'"

"They measure nails not by size but by how many you got for a penny 100 years ago."

A SHEDMAN AMONG SHEDMEN

When John's first poetry collection, "The Nutter in the Shrubbery" was published, he had no idea that just months later he would be running school workshops and performing at festivals as his alter-ego Shedman…

It all began when he entered an Arts Council competition for a placement in a place of architectural interest. A fan of Brighton's Booth Museum, John discovered that it was classed as both a listed building and a shed, because it originally stood next to the Booth family home. And so, he suggested he'd work in a shed within Booth's shed. Needless to say he won, and soon found himself stacked out with people coming to see him.

Requests for Shedman's services followed and he has since performed everywhere from a quayside to a school library. "It was a boy's school, and the teachers were amazed because I actually got the kids writing." John thinks he might be getting a bit obsessed. A shed even features in his audio-book for children "Dangerous Territory", the story of a disabled lad trying to save his pet llamas.

"The next thing is for me to live in the shed for two weeks."

A SHED IN PROGRESS

Dave started off with a vacant allotment plot and a vague idea of what he wanted his allotment shed to look like. "That's the starting point for everything – the shed." But so many friends got involved that he found the design changing day by day... "Everybody had their input."

His original idea was to have a large veranda on the shed and a bit of decking to sit out on. Now the plan is to have a herb and veg garden to the left, and to the right a decked area, gazebo, chair swing and industrial-sized barbecue to keep the troops, like Peter and Craig here, entertained throughout the summer months.

Dave confesses he isn't particularly green-fingered – "I'm absolutely numb at growing. I don't know anything." But the main objective is leisure, and the trading of traffic for wildlife, exhaust fumes for fresh air. The rest he's learning as he goes. "One guy's motto is 'Just make sure you've got somewhere to keep the beer cold.'" Dave's got a big cool box... "That'll be a feature at some point."

"The beer will probably get in the way in the summer."

BRIAN'S LOFT CONVERSION

A nine-year-old Brian was asked to look after his young mate's pigeons when he went on holiday. It was the beginning of a love affair that is still going strong half a century on. These days, Brian is at the top of his field, with regular success in National Flying Club races, and an expert on the science behind the sport. "I can predict it more now. I can tell what a pigeon is in terms of whether its character will do 500 miles or whether its character will do 700. And there is a big difference."

Breeding is crucial to success, but then there's training and diet – "Maize for sprints, peanuts for the longer distance" – and the pigeons' very own Olympic village. The loft-shed would cost a small fortune in London. Brian designed the mock-Tudor façade on the principle that light colours reflect the sun and keep the interior cool, and also on the principle that blending it in with the surrounding architecture would keep the neighbours happy. For really hot days, the ceiling moves to regulate the temperature…

"It's the working man's horse-racing."

THE SHED AT THE END OF THE ROAD

It's a common occurrence in smaller villages for one person to combine a number of trades as there is less demand for one particular service. Peter, owner of Langmaid & Hunking, is the local builder-cum-undertaker, and runs the business from a two-storey, former fisherman's shed. "There's not enough work to do funeral directing all the time. I normally do about 15 to 20 funerals a year."

Peter has been with the company for 25 years and can still remember his first undertaking in the world of undertaking. "It was certainly a bit nerve-racking the first time Mr Langmaid said to me that somebody had died in the village and would I be able to go up with him and lend a hand."

They used to get the wood from a nearby mill and build the coffins in the shed. These days, however, Peter orders in the coffin shells and fits them out with the lining and furniture. But what remains is the personal touch. "It makes a difference to people that I'm local, that they know me."

"I'm there 20 minutes doing the job, and then for another hour talking about the person."

GONNA START A REVOLUTION FROM MY SHED

At the shed-quarters of Cappella Archive, David is waging a war on inferior paper and binding, and the waste of over-printing. "Modern printing techniques allow books to be printed one at a time, as they are ordered." He uses his own "print on demand" system, which means he can produce quality editions in-house, one at a time, hundreds of times faster than the average person can read them.

In a former life he was an A–level teacher and, after years of "trying to set damp students alight on the hearth of English Literature", he took early retirement to pursue his passion for books in a more physical manner. The shed has been his base since the early days, as he wasn't allowed to keep the machines in the house.

All of the books he produces are commissioned, such as historical reproductions for local bookshops; some are more unusual, like the anglicised version of a French novel about Jack the Ripper, first published in 1935. "We had to pay £200 for a rather tatty paperback, which we then translated."

"We do everything from the printing to the cloth binding."

THE DRINK AND DREAM TEA-SHED

Tony's had an eye for follies since he was a young lad, particularly 18th-century ones with an oriental flavour. He was so inspired by them that it was only a matter of time until he brought one home.

One seemingly normal day, Tony was dutifully clearing brambles from the bottom of the garden, while trying to think up a special present for his wife's birthday. Having finally bagged up the mess, he had a sheddist epiphany – here at last, was a teahouse-sized space. So, with room and reason enough, he enlisted the help of a friend to make his long-held dream a reality.

Like Tony, the shed's not just a pretty face. Take the mural on the back wall, for example: Tony's an Englishman, his wife's Danish – so he painted the English and Danish delegations, which stand side by side in Canton, flying the countries' national flags. Then there's the way he located the shed so that it suddenly creeps up on you three quarters of the way down the garden. "It's a nice surprise in an 18th century way."

"It should really have water around it, but the ditch is still undug."

PENNY'S ROYAL TEA

"The first thing blokes on an allotment need is a shed. It's where you brew up and have your meetings and that." So says Ken, who can always be found on his local plot, followed closely by Penny, faithful pooch and top-notch ratter.

The shed is home to his tools and seeds for next year's plants, plus an array of cards and certificates from numerous shows – recognition of 40-odd years' worth of growing chrysanthemums and dahlias, not to mention sweet peas, swedes, onions and leeks, turnips and tomatoes… "I can supply myself for the year with the stuff I grow. There's nowt like pulling your own veg out of the ground."

And if he's not working the plot he'll most likely be in the shed, frying up a hearty meal of bacon and eggs on the stove or brewing a cuppa for one of his visitors – and Penny, of course: "If anybody comes and I make them a cup of tea, I have to make her one too. She won't be left out."

"It keeps me going – I love it."

THE REAL STRING SHEDDY

For years, Andy was a joiner by day, a musician by night. A self-confessed "wood and guitar junkie", these days he combines his two passions – making and repairing guitars in his beloved shed. "Well, you can't go cutting up wood in the front room. And a shed gives you that freedom where you can go and have your bits strewn everywhere without getting whinged at."

Andy built the shed to fit his exacting requirements and applies this rule-of-thumb to the instruments he creates: "If you want a certain look of one with a bit of another, you basically take three or four different types and make up one you'd like." He also gets the odd unusual request, including one where someone asked him to put frets on a violin. "Your purist would freak out."

Above and beyond all that, Andy's shed is his "nice retreat", his home-from-home. "Though I don't have the makings for tea and coffee in the shed – I have to go down the house for that."

"You've got to have a shed."

THE VIEW FROM THE WITCHHOUSE

When the original witchhouse was built in the mid-1700s, the then owner of Hestercombe House in Somerset – one Coplestone Warre Bampfylde – was creating a fantasy garden. He decided he wanted a special garden building with a seat from which to gaze at the central water-feature – a 50-foot waterfall called the Great Cascade – and witches and grottoes were all the rage... so he settled on a "witchhouse". "It was nothing to do with black magic," says Philip. "It was just a bit of fun."

The magic came later. By the 1990s, the witchhouse and the garden were all but forgotten, swallowed up by time and densely overgrown woodland. It was Philip's chance discovery of the hidden garden that set him on the long and arduous path of restoration. As for the witchhouse, it may never have been rebuilt, had someone not rolled up at Hestercombe one day with a magazine from 1906, which featured a photograph of the mysterious building. Armed with the photograph and a description from 1761, Philip and co. were able to find the exact spot where the original witchhouse stood. The rest is history.

"Children just love it."

A SHEDFUL OF HISTORY

Nick's love affair with the soda siphon began with a red, teardrop-shaped gem he found in a charity shop. "The attraction was in the design – there's that law of aesthetics where anything designed to be maximally efficient is also beautiful." He also feels a desire to preserve a little bit of social heritage, a principle which applies equally to his other collections, ranging from sweet wrappers to products from the Pifco factory.

His collections featured in a reality TV show in which a team of experts "de-clutter" your house. "We walked in with our eyes closed – the classic set-up. When we opened them, everything was lovely and empty..." But when the cameras stopped rolling, it transpired that the crew had 25 full boxes in the van outside.

So he got a shed. A right beauty she is too – maximal *and* efficient. He's even lined it to keep things nice and cosy in winter. But a shed can only offer so much help. "The theory is that every time I go to a collectors' fair, I sell. But when I go to a car boot, I end up buying again, although the ratio is much better than it was."

"It was taking up the bedroom. It was a bit embarrassing really."

...OH, AND HOW'S THE SHED?

Dave moved into his house just over two years ago. Imagine his dismay when he turned up in his removal van, only to discover that the previous owners had taken the shed with them. After the initial palpitations, he resolved to purchase a replacement forthwith.

Friends and family took great interest in his impending shed purchase. "It's all I heard for months. They weren't saying, 'How're you settling in?' but, 'Have you got your shed yet?'" And then, once he'd installed the shed, the same people would "Pop round for a cup of tea" just to see it...

It wasn't all bad though – one kind friend gave him a spider plant: "It was an offcut of their own. It's called Boris – technically the one I've got is Boris II." Boris II now sits happily in the shed, adding a bit of greenery to Dave's otherwise minimalist haven. "It's my place to get away from it all and relax, though it's a bit ironic really as I live on my own. It's nice to not have a telly or telephone or anything in here."

"I chose it from scratch."

A PAIR OF ORTHODOX SHEDS

Five years ago, Stephen left the Church of England in order to set up a Centre for Orthodox Mission with three other like-minded people, which they named the Community of St Fursey, after the Apostle of Norfolk.

Due to a reduced income, Stephen could only afford an end-terrace house with a small garden. As the group wanted to use the house as a retreat centre, they needed a chapel for the services and a library to house a large collection of religious works for the visitors to read and study. Sheds were the only answer.

The beautiful shed chapel came first – carefully modelled on a 4th-century Roman church in Silchester – and is commonly referred to as "Stephen's Byzantine Shed". The library shed followed, and is now a hive of activity, with Stephen making religious icons and producing newsletters for local market stalls. And, as it's warm and cosy, it has also become the obvious place to hold the weekly bible study. "In fact, when our priest comes, he prefers to go in there rather than in the house – he finds it more comfortable."

"It's a mini-basilica."

THE RETIRING TYPE

Some people dream of retiring somewhere hot, others want a bit of peace and quiet. Tony wanted both. A computing communications manager for a large company, he found his job getting increasingly stressful as his team was gradually whittled away. He wasn't happy, so he made plans and got out when he could.

Tony now divides his leisure time between charity work, volunteering on the Bala Lake railway and his shed, where he makes beautifully-painted wooden cartoon characters – from the small ones you see here right up to 6-foot-plus monsters – in addition to toys and the occasional less fun, practical object, like a bookcase. It keeps him happy and makes a lot of other people happy too. "I'm like a tortoise," he says. "My shed's somewhere I can go and shrink into my shell."

But, unlike a tortoise, he avoids the need for hibernation by spending the winter months in his other shed in Florida. "I do the same thing out there. Though they like wooden palm trees."

"I planned my retirement about 20 years before I retired."

49

YOU NAME IT, HE'S GOT IT

Some 19 years ago, Frank and family bought a derelict farm complete with barn and cowsheds and set about turning the outhouses into a place to display a lifetime's worth of collections. "We used to live in a little bungalow, and I put sheds up in the garden to store it all in. The spare rooms were full and I had to climb over stuff to get in the bed."

Walton House Museum has now been open to the public for 11 years. Each of his eight different sheds has its own theme, like "1940s kitchen" or "printing works". "We've got military, motoring, household, Victorian, nursery, dairy…" His current favourite is his collection of over 50 road rollers. He sources them from around the country, rejuvenating them with parts made in his blacksmith's shed, such as cast iron name-plates.

Frank hopes the grandkids will take on the museum one day. "I've got a couple of them really interested." Granddaughter Jade even has her own roller, won in a Road Roller Association competition. He's very proud.

"It's like my own little village."

A SHEDI KNIGHT

For Adrian, reading about the past simply isn't enough. He'd much rather head down to his garden shed, choose a costume and set out to do battle for the Red Wyverns historical re-enactment group and the Clifford household: "They were prominent and interesting players in the War of the Roses."

But re-enactment only goes so far. John "Butcher" Clifford would find the rules for fighting – such as no head shots – a bit restrictive. "It's probably not as dangerous as rugby, but there are risks." And not everyone gets involved in the fighting – in fact, it's a family-based activity, with an emphasis on "living history" demonstrations. Participants can choose from a range of contemporary characters, from monks to peasants to jesters, and engage in traditional activities, from cooking to leatherworking to basket-weaving.

As well as being a communal store, Adrian's shed functions as a workshop for repairing armour and making arrows. And, when he's not kitted up or fixing up kit, he's working on their website, www.red-wyverns.co.uk.

"When we first started doing it all my stuff fitted in a bag."

BETWEEN A TREE AND A HARD PLACE

Chris and Nick have always shared a shed fascination – as boys they curtained off half of Nick's dad's shed to create a unique meeting place: "Many a winter's evening was spent huddled around an old oil lamp."

In adulthood, then, Chris was never truly satisfied with a plain 8 x 6 foot shed, so began work on his own designs. There were two problems with his garden, though – a huge bank of stone and the tree his grandmother Rose had planted 35 years ago. The first problem he solved with a trailer and six weeks of graft: his parents got a new rockery and he got the garden's full width. Now all he had to do was decide: the shed he really wanted… or the tree.

"There was no way I could cut it down. The only solution was to re-design the shed." And with help from mates Melvyn, Gary, Dave and Nick, and refreshments from fiancée, Beryl, the drawing became reality, hastening a return to the shed, 40 years on, to discuss life over coffee and roll-ups.

"Bliss."

PEOPLE IN GRASS HOUSES...

Gary and his girlfriend wanted a garden workshop but they needed to keep costs down. Gary was reading a book on eco-design, which featured a number of buildings with turfed roofs... "And what could be cheaper than a few planks, a bit of boarding and some soil from the garden?"

By the time it became apparent that it was going to be both more complex and expensive, it had become a challenge. The shed was initially planned as a light wooden structure but is now much more like a bunker. "I did think about putting some camouflage netting on it but I'm not sure how that'll go down."

He hasn't had to trim the grass yet. "I bought seed that said on it, 'Resists Birds'. Basically that was a lie. It was bird *food*." But then the cat began to use the roof as a bed. This got rid of the birds but the cat created its own mess, so Gary doused the turf in cat repellent. "The problem is I hate the stuff. It's keeping me away from the shed too."

"I'm not going up there every couple of weeks with the mower..."

THE LURE OF THE SEA

Jim's father and grandfather were shrimp fishermen but, being his own man, he became an engineer. Over the years, however, he found himself drawn back to the coastal waters of his youth and the family business.

The training came in handy too. In the quest to trawl ever deeper for the tasty little crustaceans, Jim helped turn an ex-Army four-wheel-drive wagon into the Daddy of all shrimping vessels – a prototype for the vehicle he is using today. Similarly, when he set up Southport Potted Shrimps with wife Elizabeth in 1980, he applied his analytical skills to developing their own recipe. "I went around buying up all the potted shrimps I could find and I didn't like any of them." So he took the original mid-19th-century recipe and developed it to please his own tastebuds.

The shed – now the company HQ – came later, the awards and commendations soon after that. In fact, demand's grown so much that Jim's developing the dot.com side of things – see www.pottedshrimp.co.uk.

"They're lovely on toast."

"TO ME, IT'S JUST SOMETHING I'VE DONE...

"...But to other people, it's something unusual." So says David, who's "just" transforming his shed into a narrowboat – well the inside, anyway. Every possible bit of space is decorated: the walls are embellished, painted pots and pans hang from the ceiling, even the furniture he works on has already been worked on.

As a boy, he would watch his grandfather painting the gypsy caravan they shared. This fond memory was kindled by trips on the canal years later, inspiring him to learn the craft himself. The idea for his shed came to David while he was convalescing after a triple heart bypass. "It switches me right off from everything. Until I hear a voice say, 'Dinner's ready.' And then I'm in quick, I might tell you."

It's made him quite a few friends. "I live in a sheltered block. Some of the ladies come along to visit, and Flo, my missus, says, 'Hello, you're in there with a woman.' Then my neighbour up the top, every day he says, 'I've got to come down to see your shed.' He's been here for a year but he's still amazed what he sees."

"Of course when the weather's good the missus wants me to take her out."

HOLY HERRINGBOAT, SHEDMAN!

The history of herring fishing on Lindisfarne goes back almost as far as Christianity. And, just as without Christ there would be none of the island's glorious religious monuments, without the humble herring there would be none of its awe-inspiring boatsheds, like the one George is fortunate enough to look after.

Relics to a former way of life on the Holy Island, the majority of the boats are now put to use as worksheds and places to store fishing equipment and "other stuff". "The bulk of the fishing finished before the first world war," George says. "My grandmother told me that, as a child, she could run along the tops of the herring barrels from what we call the Steel End to the Castle Point, which must be well over a mile."

The exact origins of the boatsheds are vague. It's not known whether the bloke who started it all had some kind of artistic vision or was simply looking for a way of putting his leaky old vessel to practical use. Either way, George is a very lucky man.

"I've got two other sheds, a old coal house, two very big lofts, and a cellar – all bunged full."

FOR THOSE OF YOU WATCHING IN BLACK AND WHITE

A shed usually precedes its contents, but not in the case of Crucible II. Says Martin, "A local college were refurbishing the staff room and selling the snooker table. It was such a reasonable price I just had to buy it." The table was stored first in the garage, then the attic, then the sitting room – "much to my wife's protest." After briefly considering an extension, they decided on a shed and set about consulting neighbours, checking with the relevant authorities and finding someone local to build the 30 x 24 foot timber structure…

Now it's up, wife and mum Maria reads the papers on the verandah and cat Faith sits on the ridge of the roof, while Martin and Dom put in a few hours of practice for the weekend when Dom plays at a club in Aldershot and competes in regional tournaments. With a handicap of 55 and a top break of 51, he's a prodigious talent. Dad's current best of 29 doesn't quite put him in the same class, but Crucible II has certainly rekindled his interest. "I've even decided that I might enter a few competitions."

"I'm accused of being a bit of a Cliff Thorburn."

MY OTHER SHED'S A MERCEDES

There's probably a correlation between the structures most men are wont to build as lads – dens, bivouacs and such like – and the sheds they go on to own in later life.

Alan – a young pup by sheddist standards – and his "bender" sit somewhere between these two states. He built the skeleton of the structure from a load of willow branches a mate had lying around in his garage. His mate's father was happy to have the branches out of the way but apparently is still looking for the tarpaulin.

Initially, the bender caused a bit of a stir on the allotment, but natural friendliness overcame a couple of the regulars who stopped for a chat. "One or two came up and said, 'Hmm that's quite interesting… What is it?'" Alan prefers its "organic" appearance to your common-or-gardener allotment shed. Similarly, in the midst of order, he opts for a *laissez-faire* approach. "Most of the plots are square and regimental but mine's a bit more relaxed."

"I do a fair bit of weeding."

THE SHED IS DEAD, LONG LIVE THE SHED

Standing like a sentinel by a stretch of windswept estuary, this towering work of beauty is the result of a collaboration between Wilf and Tony, architect and artist, respectively. "We're very proud of it as it's one of the largest public art pieces in the area, and it's much loved and visited."

Most of the visitors are keen birders who love the range of vision the 10-metre height provides them with. "The budget was only for something about 10–15 feet, but Wilf managed to persuade them that they needed something really substantial." The pair also took the boredom threshold of children into account, including little surprises for them to discover, like the dinosaur-sized wooden egg nestled inside the building.

The shed is truly wildlife-friendly, with design features such as a double-roof made of cedar – to encourage the attentions of the local bird populace. A bird even featured in the opening ceremony: the centrepiece was a huge phoenix Tony sculpted from pieces of the old shed, which they lit on the night as a symbol of renewal.

"We got a construction team to do all the dangerous stuff."

A SEAT IN THE ROYAL BOX

Welcome to The Regal, John's very own shed-cinema, where performances are held throughout the winter months to the delight of nine lucky, lucky friends. And it's a truly authentic experience – with seats and signs from Letchworth's deceased Broadway Cinema, a box office and projection room, a programme list, forever frozen in 1959, and various bits of cinema memorabilia, including a life-sized cardboard Mrs Doubtfire...

Peggy, John's long-suffering wife, visits during the brief intermission, clad in full usherette garb and conveying refreshments for all in attendance. John places the orders via the "intercom" – a baby alarm he picked up from a junk shop and appropriated. "She doesn't mind – it's all part of the fun."

A self-confessed film-lover, there is one movie John cannot stand: "The Sound of Music". Recently, however, he found a second-hand copy and, having moaned so much about it, decided to buy it for a laugh. "It was only ten quid, so I thought why not. But I've only got as far as Julie running up the hill at the start."

"Peggy puts up with a lot. I'm a little bit eccentric."

THE NEXT BIG SHED

Pete had just completed a music qualification. He was desperate to chase his dream of having his own studio, plus his drumming was annoying the neighbours – "Not the neighbours, but the next-door-but-one."

And so, he took what was a connected greenhouse and summerhouse, and set about converting it into a fully sound-proofed recording studio. It took 4 tonnes of sand for the walls and a tonne of concrete for the roof. As for the doors, "I made the framework out of three by two and then filled it full of concrete and left it to dry. I had trouble getting it in. It must've weighed 400 pounds."

Things developed from there. "I've done all sorts from rehearsals – teenagers starting out with their bands – to a string section on a heavy metal album." And it's not all hard work – he sets up the odd barbecue-cum-gig on the raised patio outside. His dad provides freshly-caught trout to chuck on the coals and they get a few mates round... "Now we've got a toilet shed to save people going in and out of the house."

"The next-door neighbours quite liked our band really."

THE SHED THAT TIME FORGOT

Just over 2,000 years ago – before Roman invaders had set foot on British soil – roundhouses like this one could be found up and down the country. The allotment on which Paul is reconstructing it has yielded fragments of Iron Age pottery and flints from the late Neolithic, and there's archaeological evidence of a fishing community and a roundhouse settlement nearby.

With the help of family and friends, Paul cleared a derelict plot and built the structure with locally-sourced materials, which would have been used originally, such as oak, willow and hazel, and began growing Iron Age crops like leeks, beans, wheatstraw, woad and flax around it. The shed even had an authentic turf roof, but keeping it dry to prevent it collapsing finally proved too much, and Paul decided to thatch it.

The aim is to invite students from schools and colleges to come down, see how our ancestors lived and learn about ceramics and metalwork technologies from the era. "It'll be like visiting a farm 2,500 years ago."

"It wasn't fun going down to light a fire in the middle of the night."

EVERY STOP I MAKE, I MAKE A NEW SHED

It's a tradition with Chris that, when he moves house, he puts up a new shed. An experienced potter, Chris uses this – shed number four – to explore a number of Chinese glazes, whilst working with a wide range of domestic-ware, stoneware and porcelain, plus floor tiles with medieval designs. He likes the idea of combining "old materials and new materials, old ideas and new ideas", a principle he's applied as much to the shed as to his craft.

The shed's certainly unique. The old materials he's used include two 19th-century stained-glass windows from a knocked down church plus 1930s doors and windows from local houses that went double-glazed. The overall design has a Georgian flavour – testament to his favourite architecture; the roof looks like an upturned boat – he used to be a boat-builder; and the verandah is borrowed straight from South Carolina – "It's perfect for a late evening beer, sitting on the rocking chair and listening to the abundant wildlife." You can almost imagine the sound of cicadas chirruping in the sunset.

"I build the biggest one I can get away with."

THE SHED MENAGERIE

Ralph's been keeping guinea pigs on and off for 40 years. He's had as many as 200 in the past, owing to their tendency to reproduce, but these days he keeps a more modest brood of seven in his allotment shed. The cast of characters includes Dennis the Menace and the Bad Lads. "The Bad Lads are brothers. They were a pair of little so-and-sos, and they automatically became The Bad Lads."

Dennis and co. share their living space with rabbits and pigeons, but at 81 feet long, the shed affords them ample room. As the shed stands 2 feet off the ground, it also protects them from the occasional floods of rainwater and sewage that blight the allotments after downpours.

Ralph has the slightly smaller "tea shed" next door. "You get the fire going and everybody turns up." There are no further sheds in the pipeline though. "I've finished expanding now – there's no more room. Between the sheds, the two greenhouses and the chicken shed, you have to grow a certain amount of vegetables."

"They're the best pets a kid could have."

A FAMILY TREEHOUSE

Martin's grandkids loved playing in the wood and the river he's lucky enough to have in his back garden. They wanted to play in the trees too, so he installed a two-storey tree-shed, complete with bunk beds, water and electricity, connected to platforms in other trees by rope bridges, which overlook the river. "We build boats and have races – HMS Grandad and HMS Oliver." The tree-shed looks like something out of a fairytale, and not surprisingly the grandkids love it almost as much as Martin.

Selling up his business a few years back, he now devotes his energies to the things that matter most to him – the family and his charity. And so, when the kids aren't visiting, he can probably be found researching the family genealogy, or working on behalf of the Zambian Lubwe project (see www.lubwe-hospital.org.uk).

It all takes up rather a lot of time. Between Zambia, the family tree and the grandkids, there just aren't enough hours in the day.

"Probably their biggest passion is throwing stones in the river."

"I'VE NEVER BEEN BORED IN MY LIFE"

There are blacksmiths and then there are fabricators – lesser-skilled tradesmen who simply take mass-produced components and weld them together. Steve, the brains and brawn behind Ironshed (www.ironshed.co.uk), is passionately of the former category. "As you drive around you'll see a lot of hideous gates, and they're probably the same the country over. When you see a blacksmith's work, you can identify it from certain flourishes – it's like a signature."

For years, Steve divided his time between his day job and his band. While the music's still there in the background, he now gets his kicks from metal of a physical kind: "In the morning, I go outside to the shed and it's just a load of flat strips. By the evening something exists. It's very tangible, what you've achieved."

Steve also teaches, has a recording studio, is into motorbikes and has recently taken up flying microlight aircraft… "Life's just a little bit on the short side to fit it all in."

82

"I've had a crack at most hobbies in my time."

I LOVE THE SMELL OF TEAK IN THE MORNING

"It takes me right back to my school days and working on the lathe, and into my own shed there." But it's not just the smell of the wood that holds such memories for Stuart: it's the feel, the shine, the colour of the grain and the process of crafting objects of use and beauty, be they bowls or walking sticks, or the stools he once fashioned from two old beer barrels.

He's had a passion for wood and sheds since the tender age of 14, when he added an 8-foot extension to his father's shed, which itself had been built by his grandfather. He ran power out to the building, and acquired a woodworking bench that he still uses today.

And it seems that Stuart's sheddist tendencies have been passed down. "My son will go in and use the tools and all the rest of it, and now my eldest grandson, Tom, has started. He was there last Sunday, and he said, 'Granddad, what are we going to make?'"

"If he gets a shed, he'll be a fifth generation sheddist."

"WHAT'S THE POINT OF DOING EASY THINGS?"

Science is primarily based on the idea of taking things to bits in order to understand them, technology on building a machine to do a certain task. Steve's work in the field of artificial intelligence is slightly different. "I'm trying to understand the brain by building one. I'm taking an engineer's approach to science."

Three years ago, he set himself up in his shed and began work on Lucy the robot, and has since begun making a more efficient version of her – Lucy 2 – with the help of Lottery funding. As Lucy is based on an orangutan, she has already learnt to recognize bananas and Steve says she has attained the intelligence level of a frog.

Her organs are fairly straightforward – her eye is a TV camera, for example – but the brain is a bit more complicated. As making biological nerve cells is currently beyond science and transistors are nothing like nerve cells, Steve has had to create cells virtually – inside a computer. "Then you have to try and figure out how to put those neurons together in ways that can learn to think – and that's the tricky bit."

"It's hard to be intelligent when you're built out of junk."

THE REASON THE PUBS ARE EMPTY

Rick, John and Peter love their local… The beer's cheap and plentiful, there are no crowds at the bar and no last orders bell, they get to choose what music is played and what match gets shown on the television, there's no dress code, no smoking, no trouble and the comfy seat is always free.

They've been meeting in Rick's shed – the 179 Club – for seven years now. It was a humble 10 x 8 foot job, to which he added three old double-glazed windows to the front to get a bit of light in and a mirror on the back wall… "It makes the place look a bit bigger." He then hooked up a TV aerial to the side of the greenhouse, camouflaging it with plastic flowers.

Wife Janet's quite happy with the arrangement, as she hasn't got three blokes in the lounge, drinking cans of beer and knocking them over on the carpet, and they can watch the football and scream and shout to their hearts' content, or simply put the world to rights over a couple of cans.

"The neighbours don't like it when we score a goal."

HOME IS WHERE THE SHED IS

Most men are content with simply having a shed or two at the bottom of the garden. Tony liked the idea of sheds so much, however, that he has extended them to his domestic arrangements. He lives in a barn, dividing his home between that and some of the smaller outlying sheds, which house everything from the toilet to the telephone. This structure allows him to break up the daily routine. "They're like a number of different nests, different worlds I can escape into."

In a former life, one of the sheds was a 40-foot-long single-decker bus, in which he took his children on holiday to Spain and on a tour of London. After it broke down in his yard, Tony decided he actually quite liked it there, added a trellis and began to use it as a kitchen. There's a practical reason for this, too – he hates the smell of cooking in the house: "It brings back memories of old Christmases with all my aunts and uncles, boiled cabbage and sprouts."

"We cooked bacon and eggs in it, outside Buckingham Palace."

THE NOTES OF A VISIONARY

Some years ago Ian presented a lecture on the importance of the shed in the world of buildings. "The shed has its own kind of aesthetic – one that has always been neglected in the teaching of architecture." He kept the lecture notes but lost them soon after, only to rediscover them years later… in his shed.

He's been adding to the foundation of those notes ever since, with newspaper cuttings, pictures and literary fragments. Some of these are pinned on the walls or piled on the floor of the shed, which is also home to a desk, a bed and a candelabrum. "It's a kind of dreaming place, where disparate things make something."

He's still fascinated with the way sheds present a Romantic opposition to uniformity and conformity, an opposition to Modernist edifices like skyscrapers. "Sheds are temporary structures, the kind of things people put up at crossroads, before villages and towns." And he loves the element of imperfection and contradiction, the fact that sheds are ramshackle, beautiful things.

"Sheds are outposts."

ACKNOWLEDGEMENTS

For help with research and assistance, thanks go to the following individuals and organisations:

Steve Ambrose; Johanne Baxter; John Baxter; Hannah Blake; Bernard Coote; Phil Davies; David Elton; Martin Dawes (The Star, Sheffield); Dave Elton; James Franklin (Project Films); Philip Goddard; Ruth Hamilton; Paul Harrington; Mike Holliday; Catherine Holmes; Derek Jones; Susan Jones; Philip Kolvin; Derek May; Alan Marshall; Adam Morris; Daniel Mountford; Sinead Murphy; Joanne O'Connell (Manchester Evening News); Annabel Other; Tony Paul; Geoff Porter (Lindisfarne Links); Arthur Reeder; Don Smith; Louisa Soper; James Starsmore; Simon Toft (The News, Portsmouth); Camilla Turner; Frank Westworth; Ken Whale; Brian Whitlie; Rosemary Wilkinson; Uncle Wilco.

Information on Lindisfarne, The Holy Island can be found at www.lindisfarne.org.uk.

All the shedmen featured can be contacted through the publishers.

First published in 2004 by
New Holland Publishers (UK) Ltd
London • Cape Town • Sydney • Auckland
www.newhollandpublishers.com

Garfield House, 86-88 Edgware Road
London W2 2EA
United Kingdom

80 McKenzie Street
Cape Town 8001
South Africa

14 Aquatic Drive
Frenchs Forest, NSW 2086
Australia

218 Lake Road
Northcote, Auckland
New Zealand

10 9 8 7 6 5 4 3 2 1

ISBN 1 84330 745 6

Editor: Gareth Jones
Editorial Direction: Rosemary Wilkinson
Designer: Paul Wright @ Cube
Photographers: John Baxter, Laura Forrester

Reproduction by Modern Age Repro House
Ltd, Hong Kong
Printed and bound by Craft Print International
Pte Ltd, Singapore

PHOTOGRAPHIC CREDITS

John Baxter: Cover – Front, Back (Middle-Top,
Middle-Bottom, Bottom); pp 5–6, 8–13, 20–21,
26–29, 36–39, 42–49, 52–53, 58–59, 62–63,
66–67, 70–73, 78–83, 88–93

Laura Forrester: Cover – Back (Top), Spine;
pp 2, 7, 14–19, 22–25, 30–35, 40–41, 50–51,
54–57, 60–61, 64–65, 68–69, 74–77, 84–87, 96